A Note from
Mary Pope Osborne About the

MAGIC TREE HOUSE®
FACT TRACKERS

When I write Magic Tree House® adventures, I love including facts about the times and places Jack and Annie visit. But when readers finish these adventures, I want them to learn even more. So that's why my husband, Will, and my sister, Natalie Pope Boyce, and I write a series of nonfiction books that are companions to the fiction titles in the Magic Tree House® series. We call these books Fact Trackers because we love to track the facts! Whether we're researching dinosaurs, pyramids, Pilgrims, sea monsters, or cobras, we're always amazed at how wondrous and surprising the real world is. We want you to experience the same wonder we do—so get out your pencils and notebooks and hit the trail with us. You can be a Magic Tree House® Fact Tracker, too!

Mary Pope Osborne

Here's what kids, parents, and teachers have to say about the Magic Tree House® Fact Trackers:

"They are so good. I can't wait for the next one. All I can say for now is prepare to be amazed!" —Alexander N.

"I have read every Magic Tree House book there is. The [Fact Trackers] are a thrilling way to get more information about the special events in the story." —John R.

"These are fascinating nonfiction books that enhance the magical time-traveling adventures of Jack and Annie. I love these books, especially *American Revolution.* I was learning so much, and I didn't even know it!" —Tori Beth S.

"[They] are an excellent 'behind-the-scenes' look at what the [Magic Tree House fiction] has started in your imagination! You can't buy one without the other; they are such a complement to one another." —Erika N., mom

"Magic Tree House [Fact Trackers] took my children on a journey from Frog Creek, Pennsylvania, to so many significant historical events! The detailed manuals are a remarkable addition to the classic fiction Magic Tree House books we adore!" —Jenny S., mom

"[They] are very useful tools in my classroom, as they allow for students to be part of the planning process. Together, we find facts in the [Fact Trackers] to extend the learning introduced in the fictional companions. Researching and planning classroom activities, such as our class Olympics based on facts found in *Ancient Greece and the Olympics,* help create a genuine love for learning!" —Paula H., teacher

Magic Tree House®
Fact Tracker

DINOSAURS

A nonfiction companion to
Magic Tree House® #1:
Dinosaurs Before Dark

by Will Osborne
and Mary Pope Osborne

illustrated by Sal Murdocca

A STEPPING STONE BOOK™
Random House 🏠 New York

The Magic Tree House Fact Tracker series was formerly known as the
Magic Tree House Research Guide series.

Visit us on the Web!
MagicTreeHouse.com
www.randomhouse.com/kids

Educators and librarians, for a variety of teaching tools, visit us at
www.randomhouse.com/teachers

Library of Congress Cataloging-in-Publication Data
Osborne, Will.
Dinosaurs : a nonfiction companion to Magic tree house #1 : dinosaurs before
dark / by Will Osborne and Mary Pope Osborne ; illustrated by Sal Murdocca.
    p. cm. — (Magic tree house fact tracker)
"A stepping stone book."
ISBN 978-0-375-80296-6 (trade) — ISBN 978-0-375-90296-3 (lib. bdg.)
1. Dinosaurs—Juvenile literature. I. Osborne, Mary Pope. II. Murdocca, Sal,
ill. III. Title.
QE861.5.O83 2011 567.9—dc22 2010053304

Printed in the United States of America
34 33

For Marjorie Osborne

Scientific Consultant:

RAYMOND RYE, Museum Specialist, Department of Paleobiology, National Museum of Natural History, Smithsonian Institution, Washington, D.C.

HEIDI JOHNSON, Earth Science and Paleontology, Lowell Junior High School, Bisbee, Arizona

Education Consultant:

MELINDA MURPHY, Media Specialist, Reed Elementary School, Cypress Fairbanks Independent School District, Houston, Texas

We would also like to thank Alison Brooks at George Washington University for help with our time line; Helen McGovern at the American Museum of Natural History in New York City for her kind assistance; Paul Coughlin for his imaginative photography; and at Random House, Cathy Goldsmith for her wonderful and creative design, Joy La Brack for her long hours of photo research, Mallory Loehr for her ongoing guidance and support, and most especially, our editor, Shana Corey, for her diligence, insight, and joyful enthusiasm throughout the process of creating this book.

DINOSAURS

Contents

Dear Readers,

We learned a lot about dinosaurs when we went back in time in <u>Dinosaurs Before Dark</u>. When we came home to Frog Creek, we learned even more.

We went to the library. We went to a museum. We checked the Internet.

We were being fact trackers!

Fact-tracking is like digging for dinosaur bones. You know where to look, but you never know exactly what you're going to find. And in our research, we found a LOT!

We found dinosaur books, dinosaur pictures, and dinosaur DVDs. We talked to

dinosaur experts. We touched dinosaur skeletons. We collected lots and lots of amazing dinosaur facts.

In this book, we are going to share some of these facts with you. So get your notebook, get your backpack, and get ready to visit the most amazing creatures that ever lived.

Jack

Annie

1

A World of Dinosaurs

Long ago, the world was very different than it is now. Today, all the land on earth is divided into seven continents. Millions of years ago, there was just one continent.

A <u>continent</u> is one of the earth's large land masses.

Scientists have named that ancient continent *Pangaea* (pan-JEE-uh).

Some parts of Pangaea were very dry, like deserts. Other parts were damp and rainy, like swamps. There were forests and jungles, plains and mountains, rivers and lakes.

And there were dinosaurs almost everywhere.

Dinosaurs were on earth for over 160 million years. Not all the animals in this picture were on earth at the same time.

Some dinosaurs were bigger than build-ings. Others were as small as ducks.

Some dinosaurs walked on all four legs, like dogs. Others walked on two legs, like people.

Some dinosaurs had many rows of sharp teeth. Others had no teeth at all.

But in some ways, all dinosaurs were alike.

They all were reptiles. They all lived on land. They all laid eggs. They almost all had scaly skins. None of them had fur or hair.

Reptiles are cold-blooded, usually scaly-skinned animals. Snakes, turtles, and lizards are reptiles.

Dinosaurs
Reptiles
Lived on land
Laid eggs
Scaly skin
No fur or hair

The Age of Reptiles
Scientists think that the first dinosaur hatched over 225 million years ago. They say almost all the dinosaurs died about

65 million years ago. That means there were dinosaurs on earth for more than 160 million years!

Almost all the dinosaurs lived during what is called the *Mesozoic* (mez-uh-ZO-ick) *Era*. Scientists also call this time the "Age of Reptiles" or the "Age of Dinosaurs."

Scientists divide the Mesozoic Era into three parts, or periods. The first is the *Triassic* (try-AA-sick) *Period*. The middle is the *Jurassic* (jur-AA-sick) *Period*. The last is the *Cretaceous* (krih-TAY-shus) *Period*.

Different kinds of dinosaurs lived in each period. The ones we know best today lived during the Jurassic and Cretaceous periods. That's over 60 million years before the first human was born.

So how can we know about these dinosaurs

if no human has ever actually seen one?

We know about them because they left

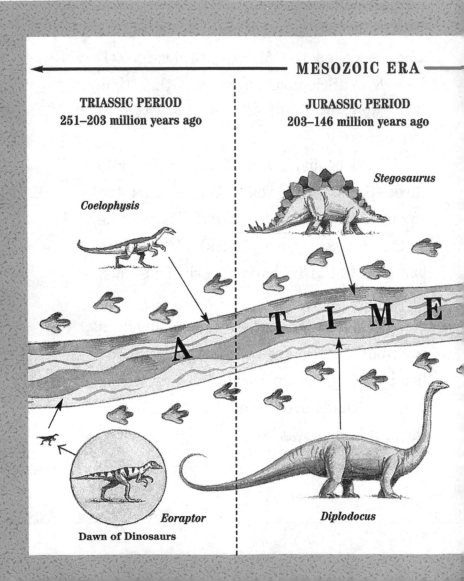

MESOZOIC ERA

TRIASSIC PERIOD
251–203 million years ago

JURASSIC PERIOD
203–146 million years ago

Stegosaurus

Coelophysis

A TIME

Eoraptor
Dawn of Dinosaurs

Diplodocus

their bones and teeth and footprints all over
the world.

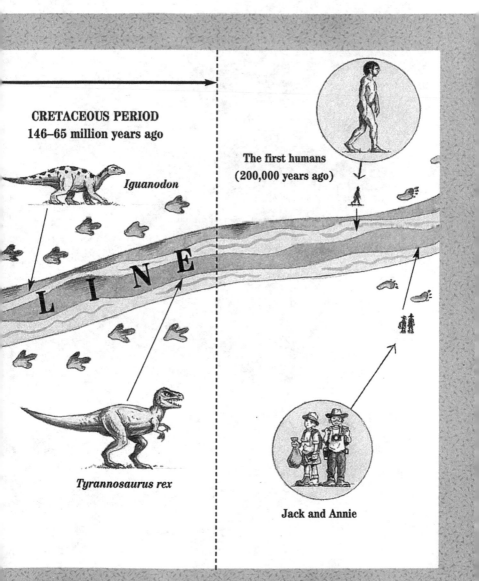

CRETACEOUS PERIOD
146–65 million years ago

Iguanodon

The first humans
(200,000 years ago)

L I N E

Tyrannosaurus rex

Jack and Annie

2

Fossils

When people find dinosaur bones today, they aren't really finding unchanged bones. They're finding *fossils* (FAH-sulz).

Fossils are any traces of life from a long-ago age.

Sometimes a dinosaur died near a stream or river. If the stream or river overflowed, the dinosaur's body would be covered by mud and sand. Over millions of years, the mud and sand turned into solid rock. And the dinosaur's skeleton was still inside!

21

T. rex fossil found in Montana.

Minerals are natural substances in the earth that do not come from plants or animals.

At the same time, water in the earth seeped into the dinosaur's bones. Minerals in the water turned the bones to stone, too.

So a dinosaur fossil is really a rock that used to be a bone buried inside another rock that used to be some mud and sand!

This is a reconstruction of a dinosaur's body that was found in an ancient lake bed.

Fossils can tell us a lot about dinosaurs.

Fossil teeth can tell us the kind of food a dinosaur might have eaten. Flat teeth are good for chopping up plants. Sharp, pointed teeth are good for ripping flesh.

People used to call anything that was dug out of the ground a fossil. (Even potatoes!)

Fossil leg bones can tell us how a dinosaur might have walked. Long leg bones are good for fast running. Short, thick leg bones mean the dinosaur probably moved slowly.

Footprint fossils can help us guess how much a dinosaur weighed. Deep footprints mean the dinosaur who made them must have been very heavy. Shallow footprints mean the dinosaur must have been a lightweight.

Footprint fossils can even tell us how

dinosaurs traveled. Many footprints going the same way mean the dinosaurs were probably moving in packs or herds. Big footprints beside little footprints mean the dinosaurs may have been traveling with their families.

Almost everything that we know about dinosaurs we know from fossils. But fossils can only give us clues about dinosaurs and the Age of Reptiles. We have to use our imaginations to picture how these amazing creatures really looked, how they lived, and how they died.

Sets of dinosaur footprints going the same way, like these, are called <u>trackways</u>.

Dinosaur Babies!

Fossils can even tell us about dinosaur eggs, dinosaur nests, and dinosaur babies.

 Some dinosaurs laid their eggs in a circle, like this.

Dinosaur eggs are usually found in nests. But dinosaur nests are not like the ones birds build in trees. Most dinosaur nests were dug in sand or mud.

Scientists say that some dinosaurs returned to the same nesting grounds year after year.

The biggest dinosaur egg fossils ever found are about the size of a football. But the mother dinosaur that laid them was over 40 feet long!

Why did huge dinosaurs lay small eggs? Scientists think that if dinosaur eggs had been bigger, the shells would have been too thick for baby dinosaurs to break out of.

He's so cute!

3

Dinosaur Hunters

The first people who discovered dinosaur fossils didn't know what they were.

The ancient Chinese thought they came from the skeletons of dragons.

Native Americans thought they came from giant snakes.

Other people who found fossils thought they came from very large elephants—or even giant humans!

In 1822, an English couple named Mary

Ann and Gideon Mantell found some large fossil teeth near their home.

Gideon took the fossils to a museum and looked at them next to teeth from other animals.

Gideon didn't see any teeth that were like the fossils he and Mary Ann had found. He decided the fossils belonged to an animal that didn't live on earth anymore.

An iguana is a large South American lizard.

Gideon thought the fossil teeth looked most like giant iguana teeth. So he called the animal they came from an *Iguanodon* (ih-GWAH-nuh-don).

At about the same time, a professor in England named William Buckland was studying the fossil of a very large jaw-bone. Dr. Buckland decided that this fossil was also from an animal that no longer lived on earth. He called the creature it came from *Megalosaurus* (MEG-uh-luh-SOAR-us). That means "big lizard" in Greek.

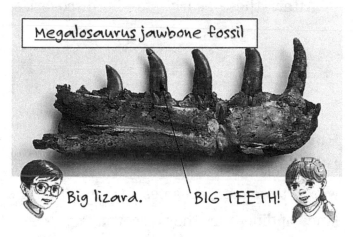

Megalosaurus jawbone fossil

Big lizard.   BIG TEETH!

Nearly 20 years later, an English scientist named Richard Owen studied the *Iguanodon* and *Megalosaurus* fossils. He could tell that both these creatures were totally different from any animals still living on earth. He decided that creatures like these should have a special name.

Richard Owen chose a name that means "terrifying lizards" in Greek.

The name was *dinosaurs*.

After these early fossil discoveries,

How Dinosaurs Get Their Names

Dinosaur hunters use Latin and Greek words to make up names for the different kinds of dinosaurs they discover.

Some are named for the place where they were found. *Alamosaurus* (AL-uh-muh-SOAR-us) fossils were found near the Alamo, in Texas.

Some are named after the person who discovered them. *Marshosaurus* (MARSH-people became very interested in dinosaurs. Scientists wanted more fossils to study. Museums wanted dinosaur skeletons to put on display. There was a race to find more bones!

uh-SOAR-us) was named for Othniel Charles Marsh, a famous dinosaur hunter.

Some are named for the way they looked. *Corythosaurus* (KOR-ih-thuh-SOAR-us) means "helmet lizard."

Corythosaurus

Sillysaurus!

The Bone Wars

Scientists who study fossils are called *paleontologists* (PAY-lee-un-TAH-luh-jists). Two of the most famous paleontologists were Othniel Charles Marsh and Edward Drinker Cope. They both were Americans who started hunting for fossils in the 1870s.

Marsh

Cope

Marsh and Cope were so eager to find new fossils that they became enemies. They hid their discoveries from each other. They sent spies into each other's camps. They even tried to steal each other's bones!

These two dinosaur hunters fought for 20 years. But their bone battles led to the discovery of more than 130 different kinds of dinosaurs.

Triceratops fossil

Discovered during the bone wars!

Over the last hundred years, people have hunted for dinosaurs all over the world. Dinosaur fossils have been found on every continent and in almost every country. Each time a dinosaur hunter digs up a fossil, we learn a little more about the Age of Dinosaurs.

Bone-Hunting Tools

Dinosaur hunters use lots of tools. Here are some things they always take along when they go digging for fossils.

Magnifying glass—
to examine small
fossils (like teeth)

Camera—to take
pictures of the site
and the fossils

Tape measure and
ruler—to measure the
size of the bones

Field notebook—
to keep a record
of the bones

Hammer, chisel, and pick—
to chip away the rock
around the fossils

Safety goggles

Water bottle

Work gloves

Sample bags—to collect
rock samples and
broken fossil
pieces

Brush—to brush
away dust and dirt

Bone-Hunter Mistakes

Even famous dinosaur hunters sometimes goof!

Oops!

The Name Game

For many years people visited museums to see a dinosaur called *Brontosaurus* (BRON-tuh-SOAR-us). But O. C. Marsh, the scientist who named it, did not realize that he had already given a different name to the same dinosaur. Marsh's *Brontosaurus* was also missing its head, so he put the skull of another dinosaur on his reconstruction because he thought the real skull would look about the same. He was wrong! Finally the name was changed back to *Apatosaurus* (uh-PAT-uh-SOAR-us), and the head was replaced.

The Wrong End

Early in his career, E. D. Cope dug up the fossil bones of a giant sea reptile. When he put the bones together, he made a *big* mistake. He mixed up the tail bones with the neck bones. And he stuck the animal's head on the end of its tail!

Horn or Claw?

When Gideon Mantell was studying *Iguanodon* fossils, he thought one of the dinosaur's claws was a giant horn. He drew a picture of an *Iguanodon* with its claw growing out of its snout!

The Wrong Robber

About 80 years ago, dinosaur hunters in Asia found the fossil of a small dinosaur near a nest full of fossilized eggs. They thought the dinosaur was about to raid the nest. So they named it *Oviraptor* (OH-vuh-RAP-tur), which means "egg robber." But paleontologists recently discovered that the *Oviraptor* wasn't stealing another dinosaur's eggs. It was sitting on its own nest to help the eggs hatch!

4

Flesh-eaters

As dinosaur hunters dug up more and more fossils, they realized there were hundreds of different kinds of dinosaurs.

Soon they started sorting them into groups. The simplest way to sort dinosaurs is by what they ate.

Some dinosaurs ate flesh. Others ate only plants.

 Yuck!

Most people call flesh-eating dinosaurs "meat-eaters." But flesh-eaters didn't eat just the meat. They ate everything—brains, bones, guts, and even eyeballs!

Allosaurus fossil

How Do We Know
What Dinosaurs Ate?

Paleontologists use clues from fossils to figure out the kind of food different dinosaurs ate.

Sometimes bones from another animal are found inside the fossil of a dinosaur. That means the dinosaur must have been a flesh-eater.

This tooth is long and pointed. It must have been a flesh-eater's.

Some fossil teeth are short and flat. They wouldn't have been good for ripping flesh. So the dinosaur they belonged to must have been a plant-eater.

Sometimes a dinosaur's droppings were fossilized. If the droppings contain seeds, it means the dinosaur was a plant-eater. If they contain ground-up pieces of bone, the dinosaur must have been a flesh-eater.

Paleontologists think all of the very first dinosaurs were flesh-eaters.

The earliest dinosaur fossil ever discovered was from a flesh-eater about the size of a goose. Paleontologists named this dinosaur *Eoraptor* (EE-oh-RAP-tur). *Eoraptor* means "dawn robber." *Eoraptor* lived on earth over 225 million years ago— at the dawn of the age of dinosaurs.

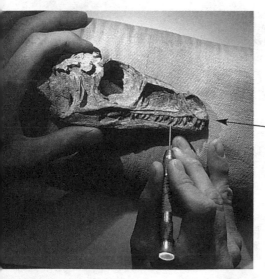

Wow! <u>Eoraptor</u> had a little head, but look at all those teeth!

Paleontologists think *Eoraptor* and other early dinosaurs probably ate insects and small lizards.

Flesh-eating dinosaurs came in many sizes. But they all had a similar shape.

The flesh-eaters walked and ran on their hind legs. They usually had small arms. Most of them had long, strong tails. Their mouths were full of very sharp teeth.

Flesh-eaters
Walked on hind legs
Small arms
Strong tails
Sharp teeth!

Paleontologists think the flesh-eaters hardly ever stood up straight when they

T. rex fossil

ran. They used their tails for balance and leaned very far forward.

Like this

Flesh-eating dinosaurs had different ways of feeding themselves. Some hunted and killed smaller dinosaurs and other animals. Animals who hunt other animals for food are called *predators*. The animals they hunt are called their *prey*.

Other flesh-eating dinosaurs did not hunt their own food. They lived off the leftovers of the predators. These kinds of animals are called *scavengers*.

Flesh-eating dinosaurs roamed the earth during all three periods of the Age of Reptiles. They were smart. They were fierce. They were fast. They were probably the scariest creatures that ever lived.

There were hundreds of kinds of flesh-eating dinosaurs. Turn the page for some of our favorites.

THIS WAY

Coelophysis
(SEE-lo-FY-sis)

This name means "hollow form."

Coelophysis was one of the earliest dinosaurs. Paleontologists think light bones and long legs made *Coelophysis* a very fast runner.

Fossil hunters in New Mexico have found dozens of *Coelophysis* skeletons on a ranch called the Ghost Ranch. Some people say that every night on the Ghost Ranch, *Coelophysis* ghosts come out and dance!

These pictures show our size next to the dinosaur's size.

Good vision

Jagged teeth

Strong "finger" claws

Long, strong legs

51

Troodon

(TRO-uh-don)

Paleontologists believe *Troodon* was the smartest dinosaur that ever lived. Its brain was very big for the size of its body.

    Troodon's teeth were smaller than a human's, but they had jagged edges and *very* sharp points.

Strong grip!

And *Troodon* was fast! Paleontologists think it could run nearly 30 miles per hour. The fastest humans can run only about 23 miles per hour.

Small teeth—but sharp!

Claws like hands

Velociraptor
(vuh-LAH-suh-RAP-tur)

Velociraptor had a long, sharp claw on each foot. It could tuck the claw up out of the way when it ran. When it captured its prey, it could bring the claw down to attack it.

In 1971, dinosaur hunters found fossils of a *Velociraptor* along with another dinosaur. The *Velociraptor* was holding the other dinosaur's skull in a tight grip. It looked like it was using its special claw to slice into the other dinosaur's stomach.

About 6 feet long

54

Teeth in rows

Long jaws

Special claws

55

Baryonyx
(BAA-ree-ON-icks)

This name means "heavy claw."

Baryonyx had a snout like a crocodile's. It had twice as many teeth as most other flesh-eaters. And it had a claw on each "hand" that was so long and sharp it was like a spear.

Many teeth

Long jaw

Spear claws

Paleontologists think *Baryonyx* must have used its "thumb spears" to catch fish. Why? Because the first *Baryonyx* skeleton ever discovered had a half-eaten fish dinner in its stomach!

Tyrannosaurus rex
(ty-RAN-uh-SOAR-us RECKS)

This name means "tyrant-lizard king."

T. rex is the most famous flesh-eating dinosaur of all time. It had sharp teeth—many were more than six inches long. It had a head the size of a bathtub. One *T. rex* mouthful of food could feed a whole family of humans for weeks.

T. rex had big, strong legs. But its arms were so short they couldn't even reach its mouth. Paleontologists are still trying to find out how—or even *if*—*T. rex* used its tiny arms.

Powerful tail

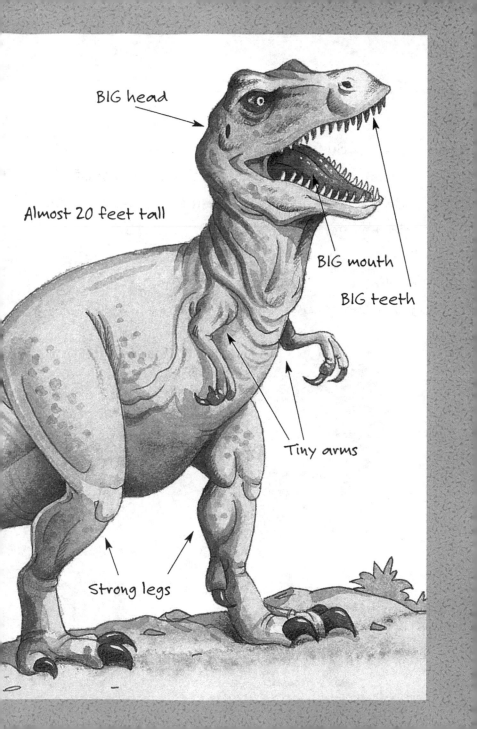

Giganotosaurus

(jig-uh-NOT-uh-SOAR-us)

This name means "giant lizard of the south."

So far, only one *Giganotosaurus* skeleton has been found. But paleontologists believe this giant flesh-eater was even bigger than *T. rex*!

Big skull

Dinosaur hunters are looking for more *Giganotosaurus* skeletons. It's possible that when they find them, *Giganotosaurus* will replace *T. rex* as king of the flesh-eating dinosaurs.

Big everything!

Sauropod fossil

5

Plant-eaters

The first, the fastest, and the smartest dinosaurs were flesh-eaters. But the very biggest dinosaurs ate nothing but plants.

The first plant-eating dinosaurs appeared on earth several million years after the first flesh-eaters. Like the flesh-eaters, plant-eaters lived during all three periods of the Age of Reptiles.

There were many more kinds of plant-eaters than flesh-eaters. Some made meals out of ferns and bushes. Others were tall enough to eat leaves from the tops of trees. But none of them hunted other animals for food.

Plant-eaters

Many different kinds
Some very tall
Some short
None hunted other
    animals

Plant-eaters
lived during all
three periods
of the Age of
Dinosaurs.

Not all these
plant-eaters lived
at the same time.

The biggest plant-eaters were the *sauropods* (SOAR-uh-pods). The sauropods left footprints as big as truck tires. They have names that mean things like "monster lizard" and "titanic lizard."

For many years, paleontologists thought the biggest dinosaur of all time was a sauropod called *Brachiosaurus* (BRACK-ee-uh-SOAR-us).

Brachiosaurus was as long as three school buses. But now, fossil hunters have found bones of three dinosaurs that were even bigger:

Big ➘

- *Supersaurus* (SOO-per-SOAR-us), which means "super lizard";

Really big ➚

- *Ultrasaurus* (ULL-truh-SOAR-us), which means "extreme lizard";

Really, really big! ➚

- *Seismosaurus* (SIZE-muh-SOAR-us), which means "earth-shaking lizard."

66

We don't know much about these giant sauropods because only a few of their bones have ever been found. But some paleontologists think *Seismosaurus* might have been over 150 feet long—as long as *six* school buses!

Was *Seismosaurus* the biggest dinosaur of all? No one knows. Dinosaur hunters discover new fossils every year. It's possible that any day they'll dig up the bones of an even bigger giant.

Turn the page to see some of our favorite plant-eaters!

Stegosaurus
(STEG-uh-SOAR-us)

This name means "roofed lizard."

Stegosaurus was about the size of a minivan. It had four long spikes on the end of its tail. It had big, flat plates growing out of its back.

Stegosaurus had a very small head. For many years, most books described *Stegosaurus* as having a brain the size of a golf ball. But paleontologists now think that *Stegosaurus*'s brain looked more like a hot dog!

Stegosaurus brain

Hot dog

68

Long tail spikes

Flat back plates

Huge body

Tiny head

69

Ankylosaurus
(an-KYE-luh-SOAR-us)

This name means "fused lizard."

Ankylosaurus was the size of an army tank—and built like one! Its body and head were covered with armor. The armor was made of bone. It protected *Ankylosaurus* from flesh-eating dinosaurs like *T. rex.*

Heavy armor —

Spikes for protection

70

Ankylosaurus had a big club on the end of its tail. Paleontologists think *Ankylosaurus* used its tail club to smash the feet and legs of any dinosaur that tried to attack it.

Tail club

Edmontosaurus
(ED-mont-uh-SOAR-us)

This
name
means
"lizard
from
Edmonton."

Edmontosaurus also used to be called *Anatosaurus* (uh-NAT-uh-SOAR-us).

Edmontosaurus had a bill like a duck's. It also had over a thousand teeth! When any of its teeth wore out, new ones grew to replace them.

Strong legs

72

Paleontologists believe that *Edmontosaurus* took good care of their babies. They protected their nests. They gathered food for the babies to eat. They probably looked after their babies until they were old enough to look after themselves.

1,000 teeth in mouth!

Bill like a duck's

Triceratops
(try-SEHR-uh-tops)

Triceratops had a face like a scary Halloween mask. It had a beak like a parrot's. It had three long horns.

Paleontologists say that *Triceratops* used their horns mostly to fight off other dinosaurs that were trying to eat them. But they also think that sometimes two male *Triceratops* would lock horns and fight with each other over a female.

Three horns

Neck shield
(called a <u>frill</u>)

Beak like
a parrot's

75

Diplodocus
(dih-PLOD-oh-kus)

This name means "double beam" (because of the shape of the bones in its tail).

Diplodocus was a long, skinny sauropod. It had a long tail and very strong legs. Some paleontologists think *Diplodocus* could balance on its back legs and its tail, then stretch up to eat from the very tops of trees.

Diplodocus ate almost all the time! Its mouth was so small compared with its body that it had to take hundreds of bites to make a meal.

— VERY long tail —

76

Small head

Very long neck

Small mouth

Strong legs

77

Brachiosaurus
(BRACK-ee-uh-SOAR-us)

This name means "arm lizard" (named for its long front legs).

Brachiosaurus looked a little bit like a giraffe. It had a very long neck and a small head. It had front legs that were longer than its back legs. But *Brachiosaurus* was twice as tall as a giraffe. And its nostrils were on the top of its head!

Strong, thick tail

78

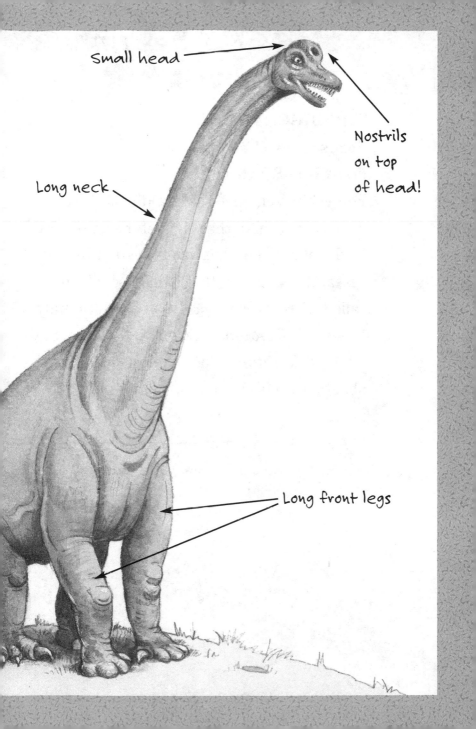

Small head

Nostrils on top of head!

Long neck

Long front legs

THE BIGGEST HEAD
Torosaurus (Triceratops)
(TOAR-uh-SOAR-us)

For years, scientists said a dinosaur called *Torosaurus* had the biggest head of any land animal that has ever lived. But new research suggests that what people once called *Torosaurus* was really just a fully grown *Triceratops*. Scientists think the adult *Triceratops*'s head must have been about a third the size of its whole body.

If Annie's head were a third the size of her body, she would look like this:

THE LONGEST NECK
Mamenchisaurus
(mah-MENCH-ih-SOAR-us)

Mamenchisaurus was also a plant-eater. It had the longest neck of any of the dinosaurs. *Mamenchisaurus*'s neck was about 33 feet long. That's nearly half the length of its entire body.

If Jack's neck were half the length of his body, he would look like this:

THE BIGGEST EYES
Dromiceiomimus
(drom-uh-SEE-uh-MIME-us)
Dromiceiomimus was a flesh-eater. It was about the size of an ostrich and had eyeballs as big as oranges.

If Annie's eyes were as big as oranges, she would look like this:

THE LONGEST NAME

Micropachycephalosaurus

(MY-cro-PACK-ee-SEF-uh-lo-SOAR-us)

Micropachycephalosaurus was a small plant-eater discovered in China. Its long name means "tiny (*micro*), thick (*pachy*), head (*cephalo*) lizard (*saurus*)."

His real name is <u>Glassesandbackpackboy</u>.

6

Sea Monsters and Flying Creatures

Dinosaurs ruled the earth during the Age of Reptiles. But they weren't the only creatures around. Dinosaur hunters have also found fossils of many strange flying and swimming reptiles that lived at the same time.

These flying reptiles are called *pterosaurs* (TEH-ruh-soars). *Pterosaur* is Greek for "winged lizard."

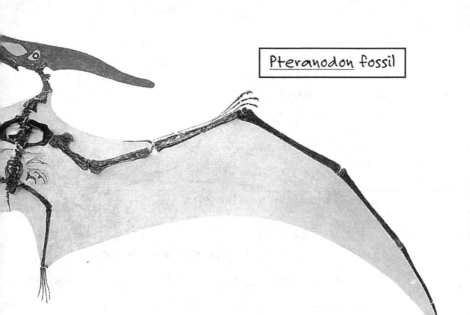

Pteranodon fossil

Pterosaurs had wings made of skin and bone. Each wing was attached to a very long "finger." The finger stretched all the way from the pterosaur's "hand" to the tip of its wing. Sometimes the finger was more than ten feet long!

Paleontologists think most pterosaurs "flew" by stretching out their wings and floating on the wind.

Flying Reptiles (Pterosaurs)
Wings made of skin
Long "fingers"
Floated on the wind

There were also several types of swimming reptiles during the Age of Dinosaurs.

Ichthyosaurs (ICK-thee-uh-soars) had long beaks and looked like big-eyed dolphins.

Mosasaurs (MOZE-ah-soars) looked like giant swimming lizards with long toes and webbed feet.

Plesiosaurs (PLEE-zee-uh-soars) did not look like *anything* on earth today.

Some plesiosaurs had short necks and long jaws, like crocodiles. Others had long necks and small heads, like the giant sauropod dinosaurs.

Sea Reptiles

Ichthyosaurs

Mosasaurs

Plesiosaurs

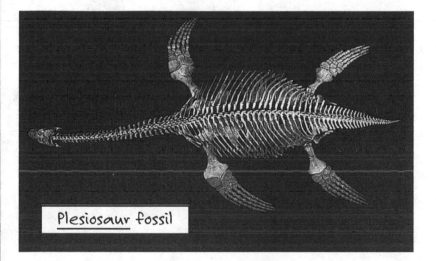

Plesiosaur fossil

Turn the page to see some of our
favorite flying creatures
and sea monsters
in action!

THIS WAY

No teeth

Stubby tail

Big wings

Flying Creatures

Pteranodon

(teh-RAN-uh-don)

Pteranodon had a long beak and a long, bony crest on the back of its head. It probably needed the crest to help balance its beak when it was swooping down to catch fish.

This name means "toothless flier."

Huge wings!

Quetzalcoatlus

(KET-sal-ko-AHT-lus)

Quetzalcoatlus was the largest creature that has ever flown. Each of its wings was about 20 feet long—as big as a small airplane's!

This name means "plumed serpent."

Swimming Creatures

Ophthalmosaurus
(ahf-THAL-muh-SOAR-us)

Ophthalmosaurus was an ichthyosaur with very large eyes. Paleontologists think its big eyes helped it see in dark ocean water.

This name means "eye lizard"

Big eyes

90

Elasmosaurus

(ee-LAZ-muh-SOAR-us)

Elasmosaurus was a plesiosaur. *Elasmosaurus*'s neck made up more than half the length of its entire body.

Paleontologists say *Elasmosaurus* may have hunted for food by swimming around with its neck sticking out of the water, looking for fish near the surface.

This name means "plated lizard."

Small head

Long neck

Flippers

7

What Happened to the Dinosaurs?

Dinosaurs lived on earth for millions and millions of years. Then almost all of them vanished completely.

What happened? Why did they die? No one really knows for sure.

Scientists call an explanation that has been well tested a *theory*. There are a few theories that explain why dinosaurs are no longer on earth.

The Changing Climate Theory

For many years, most paleontologists thought the dinosaurs disappeared very slowly. They thought they died out because of *climate changes*.

Climate is the usual weather of a place.

Paleontologists who accept this theory think that the earth's climate began to change at the end of the Age of Reptiles. As the climate changed, the world of the dinosaurs changed, too.

Paleontologists who agree with the changing climate theory say that many dinosaurs couldn't adapt to the changes.

They think that over the years, more and more dinosaurs died, until there were none left. They had become *extinct*.

Extinct means "no longer living on earth."

The Asteroid Theory

The changing climate theory was popular

94

for a long time. But many paleontologists now have another theory. They think the dinosaurs were wiped out much faster. Their theory is called the *asteroid theory.*

An *asteroid* is a rock from outer space. Paleontologists who support the asteroid theory say a big asteroid hit the earth at the end of the Age of Reptiles. They think the asteroid was over five miles wide.

Wow! That's as big as a whole town.

An asteroid that size would kill all the animals within hundreds of miles of where it landed. When it hit the earth, it would send a giant cloud of dust and smoke and ash flying into the air.

The cloud would stay in the air for years. It would block out most of the sunlight.

Without sunlight, the earth would get

colder. Plants would die. Some dinosaurs would freeze to death. Others would starve. Soon they would all be gone.

For many years, paleontologists who accepted the asteroid theory wondered where the giant asteroid might have hit the earth.

Now they think they have found the spot.

A <u>crater</u> is a dent in the earth.

Scientists have discovered a crater in the Gulf of Mexico. The crater is 120 miles wide. It is buried half a mile deep in the earth under the ocean.

The crater is full of the same kinds of minerals that have been found where smaller asteroids have landed.

Today, most paleontologists agree with the asteroid theory. But it still has not been proven completely.

We may never know for sure why so many dinosaurs vanished from the earth. The death of these strange and wonderful creatures is one of the biggest mysteries of all time.

Turn the page for more dinosaur mysteries.

More Dinosaur Mysteries

Paleontologists have been studying dinosaur fossils for almost 200 years. But there are some things they still wonder about. . . .

Case #1: Seeing Red!

What color were dinosaurs? Were they brown and gray? Or were they bright red? Green? Yellow? Were they spotted? Did they have stripes?

Most fossils can't answer these questions. But many paleontologists think dinosaurs might have been as colorful as today's lizards and snakes.

Case #2: An Age-old Riddle

How many years did a dinosaur live? Ten years? Thirty years? No one knows for certain. Many paleontologists think some dinosaurs lived to be over a hundred years old!

Case #3: Two-ton Tooters

What kinds of sounds did dinosaurs make? Did they roar like lions? Did they honk like geese? Hiss? Chirp? Growl?

Paleontologists can only guess, based on the shapes of dinosaurs' heads and bodies. Some dinosaurs had bony tubes on their skulls. Paleontologists think they might have tooted their tubes like bugles!

8

Dinosaur Neighbors

Most kinds of dinosaurs are no longer on earth. But several kinds of creatures who lived among the dinosaurs are still with us.

Lizards were the favorite meal of many small flesh-eaters. Paleontologists think today's lizards are almost exactly the same as the ones that lived during the Age of Reptiles.

The first turtles were also on earth with the dinosaurs. They looked a lot like turtles today—except some were much bigger. Paleontologists have discovered the fossil of one turtle that was over 12 feet long!

That's a BIG turtle!

Archelon fossil

Crocodiles also lived during the time of dinosaurs. Most were about the same size as crocodiles today. But dinosaur hunters have found one crocodile skull fossil in Texas more than six feet long.

That means the crocodile was probably five times as big as crocodiles today!

Phobosuchus skull fossil

And a
BIG
crocodile!

The creatures today that are real dinosaurs, though, are not lizards or turtles or crocodiles.

They are small creatures you see every day. They're right outside your window or in your backyard.

They're birds!

Dinosaur Neighbors

Lizards

Turtles

Crocodiles

Paleontologists think the first birds appeared on earth during the Jurassic Period. They were a form of flesh-eating dinosaur. The first clue came when a puzzling fossil was discovered.

In 1861, workers in Germany dug up the fossil of a small skeleton. The skeleton looked as if it belonged to a flesh-eating dinosaur. But when they looked closely at the stone around the fossilized bones, they saw imprints of wings and feathers!

Paleontologists named this creature *Archaeopteryx* (AHR-kee-OP-tur-icks). That means "ancient wing." Today, the *Archae-*

opteryx fossil is one of the most valuable fossils in all the world.

Oh, man! Fossil feathers!

In recent years, scientists in China have found many more fossils of dinosaurs with wings and feathers. These discoveries have made the link between birds and dinosaurs even more obvious.

How did birds, crocodiles, turtles, and

105

lizards stay alive when so many dinosaurs died out?

No one knows.

It's another mystery the dinosaur hunters and paleontologists of the future will have to solve.

It's possible the answer is out there right now . . .

buried in the mud somewhere . . .

waiting . . .

for *you* to dig it up.

Doing More Research

There's a lot more you can learn about dinosaurs. The fun of research is seeing how many different sources you can explore.

Books

Most libraries and bookstores have lots of books about dinosaurs.

Here are some things to remember when you're using books for research:

1. You don't have to read the whole book. Check the table of contents and the index to find the topics you're interested in.

2. Write down the name of the book.

When you take notes, make sure you write down the name of the book in your notebook so you can find it again.

3. Never copy exactly from a book.

When you learn something new from a book, put it in your own words.

4. Make sure the book is <u>nonfiction</u>.

Some books tell make-believe stories about dinosaurs. Make-believe stories are called *fiction*. They're fun to read, but not good for research.

Research books have facts and tell true stories. They are called *nonfiction*. A librarian or teacher can help you make sure the books you use for research are nonfiction.

Here are some good nonfiction books about dinosaurs:

- *The Big Book of Dinosaurs*, a DK Publishing book

- *The Complete Dinosaur*, Life of the Past series, edited by James O. Farlow and M. K. Brett-Surman

- *The Dinosauria*, edited by David B. Weishampel, Peter Dodson, and Halszka Osmólska

- *Dinosaurs: The Most Complete, Up-to-Date Encyclopedia for Dinosaur Lovers of All Ages*, by Dr. Thomas R. Holtz, Jr.

- *First Dinosaur Encyclopedia*, a DK Publishing book

- *National Geographic Dinosaurs*, by Paul Barrett

Museums

Many science and natural history museums have exhibits on dinosaurs. These places can help you learn more about them.

When you go to a museum:

1. Be sure to take your notebook!
Write down anything that catches your interest. Draw pictures, too!

2. Ask questions.
There are almost always people at museums who can help you find what you're looking for.

3. Check the museum calendar.
Many museums have special events and activities just for kids!

Here are some museums with dinosaur displays:

- American Museum of Natural History (New York)
- Carnegie Museum of Natural History (Pittsburgh)
- College of Eastern Utah Prehistoric Museum (Price)
- Field Museum of Natural History (Chicago)
- Mesalands Dinosaur Museum (Tucumcari, New Mexico)
- North Carolina Museum of Life and Science (Durham)
- Science Museum of Minnesota (St. Paul)

DVDs

There are some great nonfiction DVDs about dinosaurs. As with books, make sure the DVDs you watch for research are nonfiction!

Check your library or video store for these and other nonfiction dinosaur titles:

- *Dinosaur Hunters*
  from National Geographic

- *Dinosaurs Inside and Out*
  from Discovery Channel

- *Essential Dinosaur Pack*
  from Discovery Channel

- *PaleoWorld*
  from Ambrose Video

The Internet

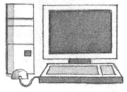

Many websites have facts about dinosaurs. Some also have games and activities that can help make learning about dinosaurs even more fun.

Ask your teacher or your parents to help you find more websites like these:

- carnegiemnh.org

- dinosauria.com

- dsc.discovery.com/dinosaurs

- enchantedlearning.com/subjects /dinosaurs

- nps.gov/history/museum/exhibits/dino/vr /virtu-quarry.html

- paleo.cc/kpaleo/dinos.htm

- paleobiology.si.edu/dinosaurs

- ucmp.berkeley.edu/diapsids/dinosaur.html

Field Trips

There are some places where you can see dinosaur fossils still buried in the earth—and dinosaur hunters at work.

If you live or vacation near one of these places, check out the fossils:

- Cleveland-Lloyd Dinosaur Quarry (near Price, Utah)

- Dinosaur National Monument (Dinosaur, Colorado)

- Dinosaur Provincial Park (Patricia, Alberta, Canada)

- Dinosaur State Park (Rocky Hill, Connecticut)

- Dinosaur Valley State Park (Glen Rose, Texas)

- Museum of the Rockies, Montana State University (Bozeman)

Good luck!

Index

iguanas, 30
Iguanodon, 19, 30,
    31, 40

Jurassic Period, 17,
    18, 104

lizards, 16, 101, 103,
    106

Mamenchisaurus, 81
Mantell, Gideon, 30,
    40
Mantell, Mary Ann,
    29–30
Marsh, Othniel
    Charles, 33, 34,
    38–39
Marshosaurus,
    32–33
Megalosaurus, 31
Mesozoic Era, 17,
    18–19

Micropachycephalo-
    saurus, 83
minerals, 22, 96
mosasaurs, 86, 87

Ophthalmosaurus,
    90
Oviraptor, 41
Owen, Richard,
    31–32

paleontologists, 34,
    36–37
Pangaea, 13–14
Phobosuchus, 103
plant-eaters, 44, 45,
    63–81, 83
plesiosaurs, 86, 87,
    91
predators, 48
Pteranodon, 85, 88
pterosaurs, 84–86,
    88–89

Photographs courtesy of:

Have you read the adventure that
matches up with this book?

Don't miss Magic Tree House® #1

Dinosaurs Before Dark

The magic tree house whisks Jack and Annie to
the prehistoric past. Now they have to figure
out how to get home. Can they do it before
dark . . . or will they become a dinosaur's dinner?

If you like Magic Tree House® #46:
Dogs in the Dead of Night,
you'll love finding out the facts
behind the fiction in

Magic Tree House®
Fact Tracker

DOG HEROES

A nonfiction companion to
Dogs in the Dead of Night

It's Jack and Annie's very own guide
to dog heroes!

Available now!

Magic Tree House® Books

Magic Tree House® Fact Trackers

More Magic Tree House®